THE LETTERS
of
CHARLOTTE BRONTË

From:
SELECTED ENGLISH LETTERS
(XV-XIX CENTURIES)

ARRANGED BY

M. DUCKITT & H. WRAGG

First published in 1913

This edition published by Read Books Ltd.

British Library Cataloguing-in-Publication Data
A catalogue record for this book is available
from the British Library

CONTENTS

CHARLOTTE BRONTË

BY G. K. CHESTERTON

Objection is often raised against realistic biography because it reveals so much that is important and even sacred about a man's life. The real objection to it will rather be found in the fact that it reveals about a man the precise points which are unimportant. It reveals and asserts and insists on exactly those things in a man's life of which the man himself is wholly unconscious; his exact class in society, the circumstances of his ancestry, the place of his present location. These are things which do not, properly speaking, ever arise before the human vision. They do not occur to a man's mind; it may be said, with almost equal truth, that they do not occur in a man's life. A man no more thinks about himself as the inhabitant of the third house in a row of Brixton villas than he thinks about himself as a strange animal with two legs. What a man's name was, what his income was, whom he married, where he lived, these are not sanctities; they are irrelevancies.

A very strong case of this is the case of the Brontës. The Brontë is in the position of the mad lady in a country village; her eccentricities form an endless source of innocent conversation to that exceedingly mild and bucolic circle, the literary world. The truly glorious gossips of literature, like Mr. Augustine Birrell and Mr. Andrew Lang, never tire of collecting all the glimpses and anecdotes and sermons and side-lights and sticks and straws which will go to make a Brontë museum. They are the most personally discussed of all Victorian authors, and the limelight of biography has left few darkened corners in the dark old Yorkshire house. And yet the whole of this biographical investigation, though natural and picturesque, is not wholly suitable to the Brontës. For the Brontë genius was above all things deputed to assert the supreme unimportance of externals. Up to that point truth had always been conceived as existing more or less in the novel of manners. Charlotte Brontë electrified the world by showing that an infinitely older and more elemental truth could be conveyed by a novel in which no person, good or bad, had any manners at all. Her work represents the first great assertion that the humdrum life of modern civilisation is a disguise as tawdry and deceptive as the costume of a bal masqué. She showed that abysses may exist inside a governess and eternities inside a manufacturer; her heroine is the commonplace spinster, with the dress of merino and the soul of flame. It is significant to notice that Charlotte Brontë, following consciously or unconsciously the great trend of her genius, was the first to take away from the heroine not only the artificial gold and diamonds of wealth and fashion, but even the natural gold and diamonds of physical beauty and grace. Instinctively she felt that the whole of the exterior must be made ugly that the whole of the interior might be made sublime. She chose the ugliest of women in the ugliest of centuries, and revealed within them all the hells and heavens of Dante.

It may, therefore, I think, be legitimately said that the externals of the Brontës' life, though singularly picturesque in themselves, matter less than the externals of almost any other writers. It is interesting to know whether Jane Austen had any knowledge of the lives of the officers and women of fashion whom she introduced into her masterpieces. It is interesting to know whether Dickens had ever seen a shipwreck or been inside a workhouse. For in these authors much of the conviction is conveyed, not always by adherence to facts, but always by grasp of them. But the whole aim and purport and meaning of the work of the Brontës is that the most futile thing in the whole universe is fact. Such a story as "Jane Eyre" is in itself so monstrous a fable that it ought to be excluded from a book of fairy tales. The characters do not do what they ought to do, nor what they would do, nor it might be said, such is the insanity of the atmosphere, not even what they intend to do. The conduct of Rochester is so primevally and superhumanly caddish that Bret Harte in his admirable travesty scarcely exaggerated it. "Then, resuming his usual manner, he threw his boots at my head and withdrew," does perhaps reach to something resembling caricature. The scene in which Rochester dresses up as an old gipsy has something in it which is really not to be found in any other branch of art, except in the end of the pantomime, where the Emperor turns into a pantaloon. Yet, despite this vast nightmare of illusion and morbidity and ignorance of the world, "Jane Eyre" is perhaps the truest book that was ever written. Its essential truth to life sometimes makes one catch one's breath. For it is not true to manners, which are constantly false, or to facts, which are almost always false; it is true to the only existing thing which is true, emotion, the irreducible minimum, the indestructible germ. It would not matter a single straw if a Brontë story were a hundred times more moonstruck and improbable than "Jane Eyre," or a hundred times more moonstruck and improbable than "Wuthering Heights." It would not matter if George Read stood on his head, and Mrs. Read rode on a dragon, if Fairfax Rochester had four eyes and St. John Rivers three legs, the story would still remain the truest story in the world. The typical Brontë character is, indeed, a kind of monster. Everything in him except the essential is dislocated. His hands are on his legs and his feet on his arms, his nose is above his eyes, but his heart is in the right place.

The great and abiding truth for which the Brontë cycle of fiction stands is a certain most important truth about the enduring spirit of youth, the truth of the near kinship between terror and joy. The Brontë heroine, dingily dressed, badly educated, hampered by a humiliating inexperience, a kind of ugly innocence, is yet, by the very fact of her solitude and her gaucherie, full of the greatest delight that is possible to a human being, the delight of expectation, the delight of an ardent and flamboyant ignorance. She serves to show how futile it is of humanity to suppose that pleasure can be attained chiefly by putting on evening dress every evening, and having a box at the theatre every first night. It is not the man of pleasure who has pleasure; it is not the man of the world who appreciates the world. The man who has learnt to do all conventional things perfectly has at the same time learnt to do them prosaically. It is the awkward man, whose evening dress does not fit him, whose gloves will not go on, whose compliments will not come off, who is really full of the ancient ecstasies of youth. He is frightened enough of society actually to enjoy his triumphs. He has that element of fear which is one of the eternal ingredients of joy. This spirit is the central spirit of the Brontë novel. It is the epic of the exhilaration of the shy man. As such it is of incalculable value in our time, of which the curse is that it does not take joy reverently because it does not take it fearfully. The shabby and inconspicuous governess of Charlotte Brontë, with the small outlook and the small creed, had more commerce with the awful and elemental forces which drive the world than a legion of lawless minor poets. She approached the universe with real simplicity, and, consequently, with real fear and delight. She was, so to speak, shy before the multitude of the stars, and in this she had possessed herself of the only force which can prevent enjoyment being as black and barren as routine. The faculty of being shy is the first and the most delicate of the powers of enjoyment. The fear of the Lord is the beginning of pleasure.

Upon the whole, therefore, I think it may justifiably be said that the dark wild youth of the Brontës in their dark wild Yorkshire home has been somewhat exaggerated as a necessary factor in their work and their conception. The emotions with which they dealt were universal emotions, emotions of the morning of existence, the springtide joy and the springtide terror. Every one of us as a boy or girl has had some midnight dream of nameless obstacle and unutterable menace, in which there was, under whatever imbecile forms, all the deadly stress and panic of "Wuthering Heights." Every one of us has had a day-dream of our own potential destiny not one atom more reasonable than "Jane Eyre." And the truth which the Brontës came to tell us is the truth that many waters cannot quench love, and that suburban respectability cannot touch or damp a secret enthusiasm. Clapham, like every other earthly city, is built upon a volcano. Thousands of people go to and fro in the wilderness of bricks and mortar, earning mean wages, professing a mean religion, wearing a mean attire, thousands of women who have never found any expression for their exaltation or their tragedy but to go on working harder and yet harder at dull and automatic employments, at scolding children or stitching shirts. But out of all these silent ones one suddenly became articulate, and spoke a resonant testimony, and her name was Charlotte Brontë. Spreading around us upon every side to-day like a huge and radiating geometrical figure are the endless branches of the great city. There are times when we are almost stricken crazy, as well we may be, by the multiplicity of those appalling perspectives, the frantic arithmetic of that unthinkable population. But this thought of ours is in truth nothing but a fancy. There are no chains of houses; there are no crowds of men. The colossal diagram of streets and houses is an illusion, the opium dream of a speculative builder. Each of these men is supremely solitary and supremely important to himself. Each of these houses stands in the centre of the world. There is no single house of all those millions which has not seemed to someone at some time the heart of all things and the end of travel.

HAWORTH

NOVEMBER 1904
BY VIRGINIA WOOLF

Haworth was the home of the Brontë family. Virginia Woolf's account of a visit to Haworth was the first of her writings to be accepted for publication (and the second to appear in print.) Woolf's article was first published in *The Guardian*, unsigned, on 21st December, 1904.

I do not know whether pilgrimages to the shrines of famous men ought not to be condemned as sentimental journeys. It is better to read Carlyle in your own study chair than to visit the sound-proof room and pore over the manuscripts at Chelsea. I should be inclined to set up an examination on Frederick the Great in place of an entrance fee; only, in that case, the house would soon have to be shut up. The curiosity is only legitimate when the house of a great writer or the country in which it is set adds something to our understanding of his books. This justification you have for a pilgrimage to the home and country of Charlotte Brontë and her sisters.

The *Life*, by Mrs Gaskell, gives you the impression that Haworth and the Brontës are somehow inextricably mixed. Haworth expresses the Brontës; the Brontës express Haworth; they fit like a snail to its shell. How far surroundings radically affect people's minds, it is not for me to ask: superficially, the influence is great, but it is worth asking if the famous parsonage had been placed in a London slum, the dens of Whitechapel would not have had the same result as the lonely Yorkshire moors. However, I am taking away my only excuse for visiting Haworth. Unreasonable or not, one of the chief points of a recent visit to Yorkshire was that an expedition to Haworth could be accomplished. The necessary arrangements were made, and we determined to take advantage of the first day for our expedition. A real northern snowstorm had been doing the honours of the moors. It was rash to wait fine weather, and it was also cowardly. I understand that the sun very seldom shone on the Brontë family, and if we chose a really fine day we should have to make allowance for the fact that fifty years ago there were few fine days at Haworth, and that we were, therefore, for sake of comfort, rubbing out half the shadows on the picture. However, it would be interesting to see what impression Haworth could make upon the brilliant weather of Settle. We certainly passed through a very cheerful land, which might be likened to a vast wedding cake, of which the icing was slightly undulating; the earth was bridal in its virgin snow, which helped to suggest the comparison.

Keighley - pronounced Keethly - is often mentioned in the *Life*; it was the big town four miles from Haworth in which Charlotte walked to make her more important purchases - her wedding gown, perhaps, and the thin little cloth boots which we examined under glass in the Brontë Museum. It is a big manufacturing town, hard and stony, and clattering with business, in the way of these Northern towns. They make small provision for the sentimental traveller, and our only occupation was to picture the slight figure of Charlotte trotting along the streets in her thin mantle, hustled into the gutter by more burly passers-by. It was the Keighley of her day, and that was some comfort. Our excitement as we neared Haworth had in it an element of suspense that was really painful, as though we were to meet some long-separated friend, who might have changed in the interval - so clear an image of Haworth had we from print and picture. At a certain point we entered the valley, up both sides of which the village climbs, and right on the hill-top, looking down over its parish, we saw the famous oblong tower of the church. This marked the shrine at which we were to do homage.

It may have been the effect of a sympathetic imagination, but I think that there were good reasons why Haworth did certainly strike one not exactly as gloomy, but, what is worse for artistic purposes, as dingy and commonplace. The houses, built of yellow-brown stone, date from the early nineteenth century. They climb the moor step by step in little detached strips, some distance apart, so that the town instead of making one compact blot on the landscape has contrived to get a whole stretch into its clutches. There is a long line of houses up the moor-side, which clusters round the church and parsonage with a little clump of trees. At the top the interest for a Brontë lover becomes suddenly intense. The church, the parsonage, the Brontë Museum, the school where Charlotte taught, and the Bull Inn where Branwell drank are all within a stone's throw of each other. The museum is certainly rather a pallid and inanimate collection of objects. An effort ought to be made to keep things out of these mausoleums, but the choice often lies between them and destruction, so that we must be grateful for the care which has preserved much that is, under any circumstances, of deep interest. Here are many autograph letters, pencil drawings, and other documents. But the most touching case - so touching that one hardly feels reverent in one's gaze - is that which contains the little personal relics of the dead woman. The natural fate of such things is to die before the body that wore them, and because these, trifling and transient though they are, have survived, Charlotte Brontë the woman comes to life, and one forgets the chiefly memorable fact that she was a great writer. Her shoes and her thin muslin dress have outlived her. One other object gives a thrill; the little oak stool which Emily carried with her on her solitary moorland tramps, and on which she sat, if not to write, as they say, to think what was probably better than her writing.

The church, of course, save part of the tower, is renewed since Brontë days; but that remarkable churchyard remains. The old edition of the *Life* had on its title-page a little print which struck the keynote of the book; it seemed to be all graves - gravestones stood ranked all round; you walked on a pavement lettered with dead names; the graves had solemnly invaded the garden of the parsonage itself, which was as a little oasis of life in the midst of the dead. This is no exaggeration of the artist's, as we found: the stones seem to start out of the ground at you in tall, upright lines, like and army of silent soldiers. there is no hand's breadth untenanted; indeed, the economy of space is somewhat irreverent. In old days a flagged path, which suggested the slabs of graves, led from the front door of the parsonage to the churchyard without interruption of wall or hedge; the garden was practically the graveyard too; the successors of the Brontës, however, wishing a little space between life and death, planted a hedge and several tall trees, which now cut off the parsonage garden completely. The house itself is precisely the same as it was in Charlotte's day, save that one new wing has been added. It is easy to shut the eye to this, and then you have the square, boxlike parsonage, built of the ugly yellow-brown stone which they quarry from the moors behind, precisely as it was when Charlotte lived and died there. Inside, of course, the changes are many, though not such as to obscure the original shape of the rooms. There is nothing remarkable in a mid-Victorian parsonage, though tenanted by genius, and the only room which awakens curiosity is the kitchen, now used as an ante-room, in which the girls tramped as they conceived their work. One other spot has a certain grim interest - the oblong recess beside the staircase into which Emily drove her bulldog during the famous fight, and pinned him while she pommelled him. It is otherwise a little sparse parsonage, much like others of its kind. It was due to the courtesy of the present incumbent that we were allowed to inspect it; in his place I should often feel inclined to exorcise the three famous ghosts.

One thing only remained: the church in which Charlotte worshipped, was married, and lies buried. The circumference of her life was very narrow. Here, though much is altered, a few things remain to tell of her. The slab which bears the names of the succession of children and of their parents - their births and deaths - strikes the eye first. Name follows name; at very short intervals they died - Maria the mother, Maria the daughter, Elizabeth, Branwell, Emily, Anne, Charlotte, and lastly the old father, who outlived them all. Emily was only thirty years old, and Charlotte but nine years older. 'The sting of death is sin, and the strength of sin is the law, but thanks be to God which giveth us the victory through our Lord Jesus Christ.' That is the inscription which has been placed beneath their names, and with reason; for however harsh the struggle, Emily, and Charlotte above all, fought to victory.

THE LETTERS
of
CHARLOTTE BRONTË

From:
SELECTED ENGLISH LETTERS
(XV-XIX CENTURIES)

CHARLOTTE BRONTË
1816-1855

TO A FRIEND
Trials of a governess

July 1839.

I cannot procure ink, without going into the drawing-room, where I do not wish to go.... I should have written to you long since, and told you every detail of the utterly new scene into which I have lately been cast, had I not been daily expecting a letter from yourself, and wondering and lamenting that you did not write; for you will remember it was your turn. I must not bother you too much with my sorrows, of which, I fear, you have heard an exaggerated account. If you were near me, perhaps I might be tempted to tell you all, to grow egotistical, and pour out the long history of a private governess's trials and crosses in her first situation. As it is, I will only ask you to imagine the miseries of a reserved wretch like me, thrown at once into the midst of a large family—proud as peacocks and wealthy as Jews—at a time when they were particularly gay—when the house was filled with company—all strangers—people whose faces I had never seen before. In this state I had charge given me of a set of pampered, spoilt, turbulent children, whom I was expected constantly to amuse, as well as to instruct. I soon found that the constant demand on my stock of animal spirits reduced them to the lowest state of exhaustion; at times I felt—and, I suppose, seemed—depressed. To my astonishment, I was taken to task on the subject by Mrs.——, with a sternness of manner and a harshness of language scarcely credible; like a fool, I cried most bitterly. I could not help it; my spirits quite failed me at first. I thought I had done my best—strained every nerve to please her; and to be treated in that way, merely because I was shy and sometimes melancholy, was too bad. At first I was for giving all up and going home. But, after a little reflection, I determined to summon what energy I had, and to weather the storm. I said to myself, 'I have never yet quitted a place without gaining a friend; adversity is a good school; the poor are born to labour, and the dependent to endure.' I resolved to be patient, to command my feelings, and to take what came; the ordeal, I reflected, would not last many weeks, and I trusted it would do me good. I recollected the fable of the willow and the oak; I bent quietly, and now, I trust, the storm is blowing over me. Mrs. —— is generally considered an agreeable woman; so she is, I doubt not, in general society. Her health is sound, her animal spirits good, consequently she is cheerful in company; but oh! does this compensate for the absence of every fine feeling—of every gentle and delicate sentiment? She behaves somewhat more civilly to me now than she did at first, and the children are a little more manageable; but she does not know my character, and she does not wish to know it. I have never had five minutes' conversation with her since I came, except while she was scolding me. I have no wish to be pitied, except by yourself; if I were talking to you I could tell you much more.

To WILLIAM WORDSWORTH
Thanks for advice

[1840.]

... Authors are generally very tenacious of their productions, but I am not so much attached to this but that I can give it up without much distress. No doubt, if I had gone on, I should have made quite a Richardsonian concern of it.... I had materials in my head for half-a-dozen volumes.... Of course, it is with considerable regret I relinquish any scheme so charming as the one I have sketched. It is very edifying and profitable to create a world out of your own brains, and people it with inhabitants, who are so many Melchisedecs, and have no father nor mother but your own imagination.... I am sorry I did not exist fifty or sixty years ago, when the *Ladies' Magazine* was flourishing like a green bay tree. In that case, I make no doubt, my aspirations after literary fame would have met with due encouragement, and I should have had the pleasure of introducing Messrs. Percy and West into the very best society, and recording all their sayings and doings in double-columned close-printed pages.... I recollect, when I was a child, getting hold of some antiquated volumes, and reading them by stealth with the most exquisite pleasure. You give a correct description of the patient Grisels of those days. My aunt was one of them; and to this day she thinks the tales of the *Ladies' Magazine* infinitely superior to any trash of modern literature. So do I; for I read them in childhood, and childhood has a very strong faculty of admiration, but a very weak one of criticism.... I am pleased that you cannot quite decide whether I am an attorney's clerk or a novel-reading dressmaker. I will not help you at all in the discovery; and as to my handwriting, or the ladylike touches in my style and imagery, you must not draw any conclusion from that—I may employ an amanuensis. Seriously, sir, I am very much obliged to you for your kind and candid letter. I almost wonder you took the trouble to read and notice the novelette of an anonymous scribe, who had not even the manners to tell you whether he was a man or a woman, or whether his 'C.T.' meant Charles Timms or Charlotte Tomkins.

TO A FRIEND
At school abroad

Brussels [c. *May* 1842].

I was twenty-six years old a week or two since; and at this ripe time of life I am a school-girl, and, on the whole, very happy in that capacity. It felt very strange at first to submit to authority instead of exercising it—to obey orders instead of giving them; but I like that state of things. I returned to it with the same avidity that a cow, that has long been kept on dry hay, returns to fresh grass. Don't laugh at my simile. It is natural to me to submit, and very unnatural to command.

This is a large school, in which there are about forty externes, or day-pupils, and twelve pensionnaires, or boarders. Madame Héger, the head, is a lady of precisely the same cast of mind, degree of cultivation, and quality of intellect as Miss ——. I think the severe points are a little softened, because she has not been disappointed, and consequently soured. In a word, she is a married instead of a maiden lady. There are three teachers in the school—Mademoiselle Blanche, Mademoiselle Sophie, and Mademoiselle Marie. The two first have no particular character. One is an old maid, and the other will be one. Mademoiselle Marie is talented and original, but of repulsive and arbitrary manners, which have made the whole school, except myself and Emily, her bitter enemies. No less than seven masters attend, to teach the different branches of education—French, Drawing, Music, Singing, Writing, Arithmetic, and German. All in the house are Catholics except ourselves, one other girl, and the gouvernante of Madame's children, an Englishwoman, in rank something between a lady's-maid and a nursery governess. The difference in country and religion makes a broad line of demarcation between us and all the rest. We are completely isolated in the midst of numbers. Yet I think I am never unhappy; my present life is so delightful, so congenial to my own nature, compared to that of a governess. My time, constantly occupied, passes too rapidly. Hitherto both Emily and I have had good health, and therefore we have been able to work well. There is one individual of whom I have not yet spoken—M. Héger, the husband of Madame. He is professor of rhetoric, a man of power as to mind, but very choleric and irritable in temperament. He is very angry with me just at present, because I have written a translation which he chose to stigmatize as '*peu correcte*'. He did not tell me so, but wrote the word on the margin of my book, and asked, in brief stern phrase, how it happened that my compositions were always better than my translations? adding that the thing seemed to him inexplicable. The fact is, some weeks ago, in a high-flown humour, he forbade me to use either dictionary or grammar in translating the most difficult English compositions into French. This makes the task rather arduous, and compels me every now and then to introduce an English word, which nearly plucks the eyes out of his head when he sees it. Emily and he don't draw well together at all. Emily works like a horse, and she has had great difficulties to contend with—far greater than I have had. Indeed, those who come to a French school for instruction ought previously to have acquired a considerable knowledge of the French language, otherwise they will lose a great deal of time, for the course of instruction is adapted to natives and not to foreigners; and in these large establishments they will not change their ordinary course for one or two strangers. The few private lessons that M. Héger has vouchsafed to give us, are, I suppose, to be considered a great favour; and I can perceive they have already excited much spite and jealousy in the school.

You will abuse this letter for being short and dreary, and there are a hundred things which I want to tell you, but I have not time. Brussels is a beautiful city. The Belgians hate the English. Their external morality is more rigid than ours. To lace the stays without a handkerchief on the neck is considered a disgusting piece of indelicacy.

To A FRIEND
Curates to tea

[1845.]

You thought I refused you coldly, did you? It was a queer sort of coldness, when I would have given my ears to say Yes, and was obliged to say No. Matters, however, are now a little changed. Anne is come home, and her presence certainly makes me feel more at liberty. Then, if all be well, I will come and see you. Tell me only when I must come. Mention the week and the day. Have the kindness also to answer the following queries, if you can. How far is it from Leeds to Sheffield? Can you give me a notion of the cost? Of course, when I come, you will let me enjoy your own company in peace, and not drag me out a-visiting. I have no desire at all to see your curate. I think he must be like all the other curates I have seen; and they seem to me a self-seeking, vain, empty race. At this blessed moment, we have no less than three of them in Haworth parish—and there is not one to mend another. The other day, they all three, accompanied by Mr. S., dropped, or rather rushed, in unexpectedly to tea. It was Monday (baking-day), and I was hot and tired; still, if they had behaved quietly and decently, I would have served them out their tea in peace; but they began glorifying themselves, and abusing Dissenters in such a manner, that my temper lost its balance, and I pronounced a few sentences sharply and rapidly, which struck them all dumb. Papa was greatly horrified also, but I don't regret it.

To GEORGE HENRY LEWES
Herself and Miss Austen

12 *Jan.* 1848.

Dear Sir,

I thank you then sincerely for your generous review; and it is with the sense of double content I express my gratitude, because I am now sure the tribute is not superfluous or obtrusive. You were not severe on *Jane Eyre*; you were very lenient. I am glad you told me my faults plainly in private, for in your public notice you touch on them so lightly, I should perhaps have passed them over, thus indicated, with too little reflection.

I mean to observe your warning about being careful how I undertake new works; my stock of materials is not abundant, but very slender; and besides, neither my experience, my acquirements, nor my powers, are sufficiently varied to justify my ever becoming a frequent writer. I tell you this, because your article in *Fraser* left in me an uneasy impression that you were disposed to think better of the author of *Jane Eyre* than that individual deserved; and I would rather you had a correct than a flattering opinion of me, even though I should never see you.

If I ever *do* write another book, I think I will have nothing of what you call 'melodrama'; I *think* so, but I am not sure. I *think*, too, I will endeavour to follow the counsel which shines out of Miss Austen's 'mild eyes', 'to finish more and be more subdued'; but neither am I sure of that. When authors write best, or at least, when they write most fluently, an influence seems to waken in them, which becomes their master—which will have its own way—putting out of view all behests but its own, dictating certain words, and insisting on their being used, whether vehement or measured in their nature; new-moulding characters, giving unthought-of turns to incidents, rejecting carefully-elaborated old ideas, and suddenly creating and adopting new ones.

Is it not so? And should we try to counteract this influence? Can we indeed counteract it?

* * * * *

Why do you like Miss Austen so very much? I am puzzled on that point. What induced you to say that you would have rather written *Pride and Prejudice*, or *Tom Jones*, than any of the Waverley Novels?

I had not seen *Pride and Prejudice* till I read that sentence of yours, and then I got the book. And what did I find? An accurate, daguerreotyped portrait of a commonplace face; a carefully-fenced, highly-cultivated garden, with neat borders and delicate flowers; but no glance of a bright, vivid physiognomy, no open country, no fresh air, no blue hill, no bonny beck. I should hardly like to live with her ladies and gentlemen, in their elegant but confined houses. These observations will probably irritate you, but I shall run the risk.

Now I can understand admiration of George Sand; for though I never saw any of her works which I admired throughout (even *Consuelo*, which is the best, or the best that I have read, appears to me to couple strange extravagance with wondrous excellence), yet she has a grasp of mind, which, if I cannot fully comprehend, I can very deeply respect; she is sagacious and profound;—Miss Austen is only shrewd and observant.

Am I wrong—or, were you hasty in what you said? If you have time, I should be glad to hear further on this subject; if not, or if you think the questions frivolous, do not trouble yourself to reply.

TO THE SAME
The argument continued

18 *Jan*. 1848.

Dear Sir,

I must write you one more note, though I had not intended to trouble you again so soon. I have to agree with you, and to differ from you.

You correct my crude remarks on the subject of the 'influence'; well, I accept your definition of what the effects of that influence should be; I recognize the wisdom of your rules for its regulation....

What a strange lecture comes next in your letter! You say I must familiarize my mind with the fact, that 'Miss Austen is not a poetess, has no "sentiment"' (you scornfully enclose the word in inverted commas), 'no eloquence, none of the ravishing enthusiasm of poetry',—and then you add, I *must* 'learn to acknowledge her as *one of the greatest artists, of the greatest painters of human character*, and one of the writers with the nicest sense of means to an end that ever lived'.

The last point only will I ever acknowledge.

Can there be a great artist without poetry?

What I call—what I will bend to, as a great artist then—cannot be destitute of the divine gift. But by *poetry*, I am sure, you understand something different to what I do, as you do by 'sentiment'. It is *poetry*, as I comprehend the word, which elevates that masculine George Sand, and makes out of something coarse, something Godlike. It is 'sentiment', in my sense of the term—sentiment jealously hidden, but genuine, which extracts the venom from that formidable Thackeray, and converts what might be corrosive poison into purifying elixir.

If Thackeray did not cherish in his large heart deep feeling for his kind, he would delight to exterminate; as it is, I believe, he wishes only to reform. Miss Austen being, as you say, without 'sentiment', without *poetry*, maybe *is* sensible, real (more *real* than *true*), but she cannot be great.

I submit to your anger, which I have now excited (for have I not questioned the perfection of your darling?); the storm may pass over me. Nevertheless, I will, when I can (I do not know when that will be, as I have no access to a circulating library), diligently peruse all Miss Austen's works, as you recommend.... You must forgive me for not always being able to think as you do, and still believe me, Yours gratefully.

TO A FRIEND
Illness and death of Emily Brontë

23 *Nov.* 1848.

I told you Emily was ill, in my last letter. She has not rallied yet. She is *very* ill. I believe, if you were to see her, your impression would be that there is no hope. A more hollow, wasted, pallid aspect I have not beheld. The deep tight cough continues; the breathing after the least exertion is a rapid pant; and these symptoms are accompanied by pains in the chest and side. Her pulse, the only time she allowed it to be felt, was found to beat 115 per minute. In this state she resolutely refuses to see a doctor; she will give no explanation of her feelings, she will scarcely allow her feelings to be alluded to. Our position is, and has been for some weeks, exquisitely painful. God only knows how all this is to terminate. More than once, I have been forced boldly to regard the terrible event of her loss as possible, and even probable. But nature shrinks from such thoughts. I think Emily seems the nearest thing to my heart in the world.

* * * * *

10 *Dec.*

I hardly know what to say to you about the subject which now interests me the most keenly of anything in this world, for, in truth, I hardly know what to think myself. Hope and fear fluctuate daily. The pain in her side and chest is better; the cough, the shortness of breath, the extreme emaciation, continue. I have endured, however, such tortures of uncertainty on this subject that, at length, I could endure it no longer; and as her repugnance to seeing a medical man continues immutable,—as she declares 'no poisoning doctor' shall come near her,—I have written, unknown to her, to an eminent physician in London, giving as minute a statement of her case and symptoms as I could draw up, and requesting an opinion. I expect an answer in a day or two. I am thankful to say that my own health at present is very tolerable. It is well such is the case; for Anne, with the best will in the world to be useful, is really too delicate to do or bear much. She too, at present, has frequent pains in the side. Papa is also pretty well, though Emily's state renders him very anxious.

* * * * *

[Tuesday.]

I should have written to you before, if I had had one word of hope to say; but I have not. She grows daily weaker. The physician's opinion was expressed too obscurely to be of use. He sent some medicine, which she would not take. Moments so dark as these I have never known. I pray for God's support to us all. Hitherto He has granted it.

* * * * *

21 *Dec.* 1848.

Emily suffers no more from pain or weakness now. She never will suffer more in this world. She is gone, after a hard, short conflict. She died on *Tuesday*, the very day I wrote to you. I thought it very possible she might be with us still for weeks; and a few hours afterwards, she was in eternity. Yes; there is no Emily in time or on earth now. Yesterday we put her poor, wasted, mortal frame quietly under the church pavement. We are very calm at present. Why should we be otherwise? The anguish of seeing her suffer is over; the spectacle of the pains of death is gone by; the funeral day is past. We feel she is at peace. No need now to tremble for the hard frost and the keen wind. Emily does not feel them. She died in a time of promise. We saw her taken from life in its prime. But it is God's will, and the place where she is gone is better than that she has left.

God has sustained me, in a way that I marvel at, through such agony as I had not conceived. I now look at Anne, and wish she were well and strong; but she is neither; nor is papa. Could you now come to us for a few days? I would not ask you to stay long. Write and tell me if you could come next week, and by what train. I would try to send a gig for you to Keighley. You will, I trust, find us tranquil. Try to come. I never so much needed the consolation of a friend's presence. Pleasure, of course, there would be none for you in the visit, except what your kind heart would teach you to find in doing good to others.

To MR. G. SMITH
Thackeray and 'Esmond'

14 *Feb.* 1852.

MY DEAR SIR,

It has been a great delight to me to read Mr. Thackeray's work; and I so seldom now express my sense of kindness that, for once, you must permit me, without rebuke, to thank you for a pleasure so rare and special. Yet I am not going to praise either Mr. Thackeray or his book. I have read, enjoyed, been interested, and after all, feel full as much ire and sorrow as gratitude and admiration. And still one can never lay down a book of his without the two last feelings having their part, be the subject or treatment what it may. In the first half of the book, what chiefly struck me was the wonderful manner in which the writer throws himself into the spirit and letters of the times whereof he treats; the allusions, the illustrations, the style, all seem to me so masterly in their exact keeping, their harmonious consistency, their nice, natural truth, their pure exemption from exaggeration. No second-rate imitator can write in that way; no coarse scene-painter can charm us with an allusion so delicate and perfect. But what bitter satire, what relentless dissection of diseased subjects! Well, and this, too, is right, or would be right, if the savage surgeon did not seem so fiercely pleased with his work. Thackeray likes to dissect an ulcer or an aneurism; he has pleasure in putting his cruel knife or probe into quivering, living flesh. Thackeray would not like all the world to be good; no great satirist would like society to be perfect.

As usual, he is unjust to women; quite unjust. There is hardly any punishment he does not deserve for making Lady Castlewood peep through a keyhole, listen at a door, and be jealous of a boy and a milkmaid. Many other things I noticed that, for my part, grieved and exasperated me as I read; but then, again, came passages so true, so deeply thought, so tenderly felt, one could not help forgiving and admiring....

But I wish he could be told not to care much for dwelling on the political or religious intrigues of the times. Thackeray, in his heart, does not value political or religious intrigues of any age or date. He likes to show us human nature at home, as he himself daily sees it; his wonderful observant faculty likes to be in action. In him this faculty is a sort of captain and leader; and if ever any passage in his writings lacks interest, it is when this master-faculty is for a time thrust into a subordinate position. I think such is the case in the former half of the present volume. Towards the middle, he throws off restraint, becomes himself, and is strong to the close. Everything now depends on the second and third volumes. If, in pith and interest, they fall short of the first, a true success cannot ensue. If the continuation be an improvement upon the commencement, if the stream gather force as it rolls, Thackeray will triumph. Some people have been in the habit of terming him the second writer of the day; it just depends on himself whether or not these critics shall be justified in their award. He need not be the second. God made him second to no man. If I were he, I would show myself as I am, not as critics report me; at any rate, I would do my best. Mr. Thackeray is easy and indolent, and seldom cares to do his best. Thank you once more; and believe me—&c.

TO THE SAME
'Esmond' again

10 *Nov.* 1852.

... I have read the third volume of *Esmond.* I found it both entertaining and exciting to me; it seems to possess an impetus and excitement beyond the other two,—that movement and brilliancy its predecessors sometimes wanted, never fails here. In certain passages, I thought Thackeray used all his powers; their grand, serious force yielded a profound satisfaction. 'At last he puts forth his strength,' I could not help saying to myself. No character in the book strikes me as more masterly than that of Beatrix; its conception is fresh, and its delineation vivid. It is peculiar; it has impressions of a new kind—new at least, to me. Beatrix is not, in herself, all bad. So much does she sometimes reveal of what is good and great as to suggest this feeling—you would think she was urged by a Fate. You would think that some antique doom presses on her house, and that once in so many generations its brightest ornament was to become its greatest disgrace. At times, what is good in her struggles against this terrible destiny, but the Fate conquers. Beatrix cannot be an honest woman and a good man's wife. She 'tries, and she *cannot*'. Proud, beautiful, and sullied, she was born what she becomes, a king's mistress. I know not whether you have seen the notice in the *Leader*; I read it just after concluding the book. Can I be wrong in deeming it a notice tame, cold, and insufficient? With all its professed friendliness, it produced on me a most disheartening impression. Surely, another sort of justice than this will be rendered to *Esmond* from other quarters. One acute remark of the critic is to the effect that Blanche Amory and Beatrix are identical—sketched from the same original! To me they are about as identical as a weazel and a royal tigress of Bengal; both the latter are quadrupeds,—both the former, women.

www.ingramcontent.com/pod-product-compliance
Lightning Source LLC
LaVergne TN
LVHW041239080426
835508LV00011B/1283
9781528704069